Looking at Literature Through Primary Sources™

The Red Badge of Courage and the Civil War

Linda Bickerstaff

rosen central
Primary Source™
The Rosen Publishing Group, Inc., New York

Published in 2004 by The Rosen Publishing Group, Inc.
29 East 21st Street, New York, NY 10010

Library of Congress Cataloging-in-Publication Data

Bickerstaff, Linda.
The Red Badge of Courage and the Civil War/by Linda Bickerstaff.—1st ed.
  p. cm.—(Looking at literature through primary sources)
Summary: Traces the process and influences behind the writing of Stephen Crane's novel, *The Red Badge of Courage*, which was published in 1893 when the Civil War was still fresh in the public mind.
Includes bibliographical references (p. 61) and index.
ISBN 0-8239-4506-5
1. Crane, Stephen, 1871–1900. *The Red Badge of Courage*—Sources. 2. United States—History—Civil War, 1861–1865—Literature and the war. [1. Crane, Stephen, 1871–1900. *The Red Badge of Courage*—Sources. 2. American literature—History and criticism. 3. United States—History—Civil War, 1861–1865—Literature and the war.]
I. Title. II. Series.
PS1449.C85R3915 2004
813'.4—dc22

                                                              2003014615

On the cover: At top, a photograph of Stephen Crane, taken in the 1890s; at bottom left, a portrait of a Union soldier, circa 1861; and at bottom right, the cover of the first edition of *The Red Badge of Courage*.

CONTENTS

INTRODUCTION

Stephen Crane's *The Red Badge of Courage* is set amid the Battle of Chancellorsville during the American Civil War. It is the story of a young Union soldier, who, when faced with the realities of war, runs from the battle. It is the story of how a boy, perhaps like many of the teenagers who fought in that war, reacts and responds to terrifying situations. It is the story of his struggle to find courage and become a hero. While some readers interpret the novel as a picture of a boy maturing into a man, others disagree. There is no doubt what the youth himself believes.

> With this conviction came a store of assurance. He felt a quiet manhood, non-assertive but of sturdy and strong blood. He knew that he would no more quail before his guides wherever they should point. He had been to touch the great death, and found that, after all, it was but the great death and was for others. He was a man.

This photograph, titled *Incidence of War—A Harvest of Death,* shows the bodies of soldiers killed in one of the many battles of the Civil War between 1861 and 1865. The Civil War and, in particular, the experiences of teenage boys who joined armies or who were called into service during the war formed the inspiration for Stephen Crane's enduring novel, *The Red Badge of Courage.*

Stephen Crane wrote the first draft of *The Red Badge of Courage* in ten days during March 1893. In late 1894, installments of the book, which Crane had shortened, were published in the *Philadelphia Press.* In October 1895, the entire novel was published by D. Appleton and Company. More than a century later, it is still in print. This portrait of one boy's struggle, painted in words by Stephen Crane, could be the picture of every boy's struggle in war.

Chapter 1

Stephen Crane's Story

S tephen Crane was a preacher's son. The youngest of fourteen children, he was born in Newark, New Jersey, on November 1, 1871. His father, Jonathan Townley Crane, was a strict Methodist minister. His mother, Mary Peck Crane, was a writer and a hardworking member of the Women's Christian Temperance Union.

Stephen Crane spent his early school years in Port Jervis, New York, where his family had moved in 1878. It is probable that the first seeds of *The Red Badge of Courage* were sown there. Veterans of the 124th New York Volunteers gathered in the Port Jervis town park to spin stories of their Civil War experiences. No boy could have resisted those tales—certainly not Crane.

Reverend Crane died in 1880. Three years later, Mrs. Crane moved the family to Asbury Park, New Jersey, where one of Crane's older brothers worked as a newspaper correspondent. When not in school or writing his own stories, Crane helped his brother gather the local news.

In 1888, Crane enrolled in prep school at the Hudson River Institute (Claverack College), in Claverack, New York. Ideas for

Stephen Crane's father, Jonathan, is shown at left in a photograph that was taken sometime in the 1870s. His mother, Mary, is shown at right in an 1889 portrait. Both of Crane's parents, as well as two of his brothers, did some writing. This probably explains Crane's early interest in writing. He began writing stories when he was around eight years old.

The Red Badge of Courage may have continued to grow there due to the influence of one of Crane's instructors, John Bullock Van Petten, a retired Civil War general.

When he entered Lafayette College, in Easton, Pennsylvania, in 1890, Crane's intent was to become a mining engineer. He spent more time cutting classes and playing baseball than he did studying, so his stay at Lafayette was brief—one semester. He transferred to Syracuse University in New York the following year but soon quit school altogether.

	Alg. 5 Per.	Chem. 4 Per.	Drawing 2 Per.	French 4 Per.	Bib. 1 Per.	Elo. 1 Per.	Theme 1 Per.	Average
Anderson	95.	90.	96.5	91.	95.	93.	96.	93.1
Beddall	85.	95.	96.8	90.	94.	94.	95.5	91.2
Breisch	93.	92.	95.	91.	95.	93.	94.	92.7
Crane, S.	60.	no grade	no grade	85	no grade	92.	0	
Dietrich	97.	96.	93.5	93.	95.	91.	97.	95.0
Griswold	95.	98.						
Hansoy	94.5	98.						
Harper	93.	90.						
Harrison	90.	92.						
Hawkins	93.	94.						

Stephen Crane never cared much for formal schooling. As this Lafayette College grade record (from 1890 to 1892) shows, Crane was an indifferent student. He rarely attended classes. However, he was a popular student who was involved in many extracurricular activities. In the inset photograph, Crane is shown *(second row, third from right)* with the Claverack College student battalion, in which he attained the rank of captain.

A Bohemian Life

After his mother's death in late 1890, Crane moved to New York City, where he lived in the slums of the Bowery in Manhattan. Rebelling against his strict religious upbringing, he was soon enjoying card-playing, dancing, drinking, and smoking—all of which his father, in a series of popular pamphlets, had condemned as evil. Because of his unconventional lifestyle, Crane began to acquire the reputation of being a bohemian.

Crane worked as a freelance writer for the *New York Herald* and the *New York Tribune* while writing his first novel, *Maggie: A Girl of the Streets.* The story of the life of a young prostitute was too grim to be accepted for publication in magazines. The novel was also rejected by several book publishers. Finally, in 1892, Crane borrowed $700 from his brother and published the book himself, under the pseudonym (pen name) Johnston Smith. He offered the book for sale at newsstands, but most of the copies remained piled on the floor of his apartment.

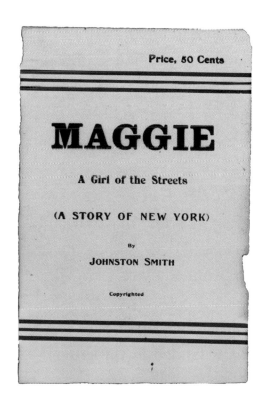

Price, 50 Cents

MAGGIE

A Girl of the Streets

(A STORY OF NEW YORK)

By

JOHNSTON SMITH

Copyrighted

◆◆◆ **This is the cover of Stephen Crane's first novel, *Maggie*, which he self-published in 1892 under the pseudonym Johnston Smith. Most critics at the time dismissed it as being coarse and unfit for polite society, but a few praised Crane for bringing attention to the harsh reality of urban life.**

Crane, broke and depressed, was about to give up writing novels when William Dean Howells, an influential literary figure, praised *Maggie* in a newspaper interview. Encouraged, Crane took up a new project.

Crane's Second Novel

In March 1893, Crane began the first draft of *The Red Badge of Courage*, which he originally named *Private Fleming: His Various Battles.* Although he wrote this draft in ten days, several months passed before he completed the final manuscript. A shortened version of the book was serialized and published in the *Philadelphia Press* in 1894. Crane was only twenty-three years old when this book catapulted him to fame.

The unabridged manuscript was published the following year by D. Appleton and Company in the United States and by Heinemann Publishing in England. Two more editions of the book were printed in 1895, and by March 1896, an additional fourteen printings had been made.

An instant success, *The Red Badge of Courage* was a vivid portrait of war as seen by the common soldier. It allowed and continues to allow each reader to see and feel what the boys and men who fought in the Civil War must have experienced.

A shell screaming like a storm banshee went over the huddled heads of the reserves. It landed in the grove,

and exploding, redly flung the brown earth. There was a little shower of pine needles.

Bullets began to whistle among the branches and nip at the trees. Twigs and leaves came sailing down. It was as if a thousand axes, wee and invisible, were being wielded. Many of the men were constantly dodging and ducking their heads.

Although he lacked firsthand knowledge of the Civil War, Crane's account of the trials of a young Union soldier was so believable that many early reviewers of the novel thought the author was a Civil War veteran. Who but a veteran could have written these words?

Others began to scamper away through the smoke. The youth turned his head, shaken from his trance by this movement as if the regiment was leaving him behind . . . He yelled then with fright and swung about. For a moment, in the great clamor, he was like a proverbial chicken. He lost the direction of safety. Destruction threatened him from all points . . . Directly he began to speed toward the rear in great leaps. His rifle and cap were gone. His unbuttoned coat bulged in the wind. The flap of his cartridge box bobbed wildly, and his canteen, by its slender cord, swung on behind. On his face was the horror of those things which he imagined.

◆◆◆ Crane's success as an author and a war correspondent made him a celebrity in the 1890s. During that time, he lived extravagantly, but he worked feverishly to produce an impressive body of writing.

In the Aftermath of Success

Because of the success of *The Red Badge of Courage*, Crane was hired by the Bacheller Syndicate to travel to the American West and Southwest, writing articles for the syndicate's paper. This trip took him through Nebraska, down to Texas, and eventually to Mexico, where he was attacked by bandits. This and many other episodes led him to write newspaper articles as well as many poems and short stories.

In January 1897, while traveling on a vessel that was carrying weapons to Cuban rebels, Crane was shipwrecked. He spent almost three days on a life raft before safely returning to the Florida shore. The experience led to his writing "The Open Boat," perhaps the most famous of his short stories.

In Jacksonville, Florida, Crane met Cora Taylor, the owner of a brothel, the Hotel de Dream. Cora, also a writer, took Crane's name as his common-law wife and traveled with him to Greece in late 1897 to cover the Greco-Turkish War. Cora submitted stories from Greece and is considered to be the first female war correspondent. Her pseudonym was Imogene Carter.

In 1898, after the assignment in Greece, the Cranes settled in Oxted, Surrey, England.

Crane Dies at Twenty-eight

Still fascinated with war, Crane took a job in 1899 covering the Spanish-American War for a newspaper, the *New York World*. While in Cuba, his health deteriorated, forcing him to return to New York to recuperate. There, he was accused of drug abuse, drunkenness, and general depravity. Disgusted with these unwarranted claims, Crane returned to England. He and Cora moved to Brede Place in Sussex, England. They were there for only a few months when Crane's health began to worsen. Cora took him to Badenweiler, a health spa in Baden, Germany, where he died on June 5, 1900, from complications of tuberculosis.

Chapter 2

The Red Badge of Courage: The Story

The *Red Badge of Courage* is the story of a boy, Henry Fleming, who leaves his widowed mother to fight for the Union army in the American Civil War. The war offers him an opportunity to get away from his humdrum life and away from his controlling mother. Caught up in the excitement of the times, he believes that fighting will be a great adventure. He believes he will be a hero.

> He had burned several times to enlist. Tales of great movements shook the land . . . He had read of marches, sieges, conflicts, and he longed to see it all. His busy mind had drawn for him large pictures extravagant in color, lurid with breathless deeds.

The regiment in which Henry has enlisted, comprised mostly of inexperienced volunteers, spends weeks camped across the river from the enemy. The constant drilling, marching, cooking, and cleaning that fills these weeks is not at all what Henry had expected. He has a lot of time to think about the upcoming battle

I was young, but not unobserving, and did not believe, from the first, in a sixty days' war; nor did I consider ten dollars a month, and the promised glory, large pay for the services of an able-bodied young man. Enlistment scenes are usually pictured as entirely heroic, but truth compels me to acknowledge that my feelings were mixed. At this

Leaving for the Front.

moment I cannot repress a smile of amusement and pity for that young recruit — myself.

It was the news that the Sixth Massachusetts

It is widely accepted that Stephen Crane referred to Warren Lee Goss's *Recollections of a Private* in preparing to write *The Red Badge of Courage.* Goss's book, an illustration from which is shown here, is a record of his experience as a Union soldier during the Civil War.

and to wonder how he will act when put to the test. When word arrives that the regiment will soon see action, Henry is afraid that he will be a coward and run away from the fight. He does not want his friends to see his fear and think badly of him.

> He lay in his bunk pondering on it. He tried to mathematically prove to himself that he would not run from battle. Previously he had never felt obliged to wrestle too seriously with this question. In his life he had taken certain things for granted, never challenging his belief

15

in ultimate success, and bothering little about means and roads. But here he was confronted with a thing of moment. It had suddenly appeared to him that perhaps in a battle he might run.

Henry Runs

The regiment is soon engaged in battle. Henry, caught up in the fury of the fight, loads and fires his rifle almost automatically as the enemy charges the Union lines. When the first skirmish is over and the enemy has retreated, Henry celebrates—believing that the ordeal is over and that he is a "fine fellow" to have endured and won. Then the regiment is taken by surprise when the enemy attacks again with more ferocity. Some of the untried Union soldiers, believing that they are outnumbered, start to run. Others follow. It seems to Henry that the battle is lost, and he, too, runs away.

Henry's worst fear has been realized. He has acted in a cowardly manner, and all of his fellow soldiers will know. As he wanders through the woods behind the battlefield, he begins to make excuses for his actions. He convinces himself that he has run in order to save himself to fight another day. He begins to feel superior to those who stayed to fight—those "methodical idiots," those "machine-like fools"—who he is sure are now dead or captured. They were not as smart as he was. They didn't get out when they could.

This drawing by Edwin Forbes depicts a key battle of the Civil War—the one that Crane is believed to have fictionalized in *The Red Badge of Courage*. Forbes created this drawing in May 1863, while he was on the battlefield.

Henry suddenly hears cheering from the battlefield. Union soldiers have held the lines and won.

> The youth cringed as if discovered in a crime. By heavens, they had won after all! The imbecile line had remained and become victors.

Henry becomes angry and bitter, and eventually begins to feel self-pity. He had convinced himself that he had done the right thing by running. Now he thinks he will be ridiculed and thought a coward by those who stayed to fight.

Henry Receives His Red Badge of Courage

Wandering away from battle, Henry encounters a group of wounded men moving to the rear. One soldier, referred to only as the tattered man, strikes up a conversation with Henry. "Where yeh hit, ol' boy?" the tattered man asks. Henry doesn't answer because he has no wounds at all.

Among the wounded, Henry sees Jim Conklin, a friend from his regiment. Jim has been shot and appears badly wounded. Henry and the tattered man try to help Jim, but he dies of his wounds.

> **As the flap of the blue jacket fell away from the body, [Henry] could see that the side looked as if it had been chewed by wolves. The youth turned, with sudden, livid rage, toward the battle-field. He shook his fist. He seemed about to deliver a philippic.**
>
> **"Hell—"**

The tattered man begins to weaken, and it seems to Henry that he might also die. Horrified by Jim's death and scared that the tattered man will find out that he is uninjured, Henry runs, deserting the failing tattered man. Henry wishes that he had a wound, a red badge, to show that he was courageous like these men.

This photograph shows wounded soldiers on the battlefield on May 2, 1863, after the Battle of Chancellorsville near Fredericksburg, Virginia.

As he continues to wander, Union soldiers suddenly appear, running through the trees and thick underbrush. Henry tries to stop one of the soldiers to get information.

> The youth, after rushing about and throwing interrogations at the heedless bands of retreating infantry, finally clutched a man by the arm. They swung around face to face. . .
>
> The man screamed: "Let go me! Let go me!" His face was livid and his eyes were rolling uncontrolled.

He was heaving and panting. He still grasped his rifle, perhaps having forgotten to release his hold upon it, he tugged frantically . . .

> **"Let go me! Let go me!"**
>
> **"Why—Why—" stuttered the youth . . .**
>
> **"Well, then!" bawled the man in a lurid rage. He adroitly and fiercely swung his rifle. It crushed upon the youth's head.**

Henry receives his false red badge.

Timeline

November 6, 1860	December 20, 1860	February 9, 1861	March 4, 1861
Abraham Lincoln is elected president of the United States of America.	South Carolina secedes from the Union, followed by six other Southern states.	The Confederate States of America forms with Jefferson Davis as president.	Abraham Lincoln is inaugurated as the sixteenth president of the United States.

"Yeh seem t' be in a pretty bad way, boy," says the cheerful soldier who finds Henry some time later. "What reg'ment do yeh b'long teh?" The soldier helps Henry to return to his regiment, where he is greeted as a hero because he has a red badge.

Henry Returns to Battle

The next day, the battle resumes and Henry finds himself back on the firing line. In the first skirmish of the day, Henry fights like a fiend, firing even after the enemy has retreated.

April 12, 1861	July 21, 1861	March 9, 1862	December 11–15, 1862
Fort Sumter, in Charleston, South Carolina, is fired on. The war begins.	First Battle of Bull Run, in Manassas, Virginia. First major land battle of the armies in Virginia.	Confederate ironclad ship the *Merrimac* battles Union ironclad the *Monitor.* Neither wins.	Battle at Fredericksburg, Virginia. General Burnsides is replaced by General Hooker as head of the Union forces.

The flames bit him, and the hot smoke broiled his skin. His rifle barrel grew so hot that ordinarily he could not have borne it upon his palms; but he kept on stuffing cartridges into it, and pounding them with his clanking, bending ramrod . . . he pulled his trigger with a fierce grunt, as if he were dealing a blow of the fist with all his strength. When the enemy seemed falling back before him and his fellows, he went instantly forward . . . once he, in his intent hate, was almost alone, and was firing, when all those near him had ceased.

Timeline *continued*

May 1–5, 1863	July 1–3, 1863	November 19, 1863	July 30– December 16, 1864
Battle in Chancellorsville, Virginia, on which *The Red Badge of Courage* was based.	Battle at Gettysburg, Pennsylvania. Largest battle of Civil War; 51,000 casualties. Union victory.	President Lincoln delivers the Gettysburg Address.	Fourteen major battles in five states: Virginia, Georgia, Alabama, South Carolina, and Tennessee.

He is praised by the lieutenant who says, "By heavens, if I had ten thousand wild cats like you I could tear th' stomach outa this war in less'n a week!" Henry is happy that he has shown his friends that he is a good soldier.

In the next skirmish of the battle, the sergeant carrying the Union flag is killed. Henry picks up the flag and carries it into the attack. In yet another skirmish, an enemy unit is overrun. Henry and a companion capture the enemy's flag. Again, Henry is praised. He feels that he is a hero and that he has earned his red badge.

The Union army eventually withdraws across the river. As the soldiers march away, Henry thinks he has indeed become a man.

April 2, 1865	April 3, 1865	April 9, 1865
The Fall of Richmond, Virginia, and the collapse of the Confederacy. Jefferson Davis flees.	Battle at Sayler's Creek, Virginia. Death knell for Confederate army.	Battle at Appomattox Court House, Virginia. Final Union victory. Surrender of General Robert E. Lee to General Ulysses S. Grant. Official end of war.

Chapter 3

The Civil War: Backdrop for *The Red Badge of Courage*

Since the surrender of Confederate general Robert E. Lee at Appomattox Court House, on April 9, 1865, the event that ended the Civil War, more than 50,000 books and pamphlets have been written about this tragic chapter in American history. Many books were written in the thirty years between the end of the war and the writing of *The Red Badge of Courage.*

Many Civil War soldiers were literate. Keeping a diary was common. Letters written by soldiers to family and friends were preserved and later published. The army had not yet begun to censor letters. Later, stories about battles, heroes, and lost friends were traded by veterans wherever they gathered and were passed along to whomever would listen. Photojournalists took their cumbersome cameras to war and preserved its realities. Artists, with sketches and paints, immortalized the men who fought.

Stephen Crane borrowed all of these pictures of war, mixed them with a large dose of imagination, and created *The Red Badge of Courage.* The story, far from romanticizing and idealizing war, tells it like it was.

The ragged line had respite for some minutes, but during its pause the struggle in the forest became magnified until the trees seemed to quiver from the firing and the ground to shake from the rushing of the men. The voices of the cannon were mingled in a long and interminable row. It seemed difficult to live in such an atmosphere. The chests of the men strained for a bit of freshness, and their throats craved water.

There was one shot through the body, who raised a cry of bitter lamentation when came this lull. Perhaps he had been calling out during the fighting also, but at that time no one had heard him. But now the men turned at the woeful complaints of him upon the ground . . . When their eyes first encountered him there was a sudden halt, as if they feared to go near. He was thrashing about in the grass, twisting his shuddering body into many strange postures. He was screaming loudly.

Pictures of War

Artist, scientist, and inventor Samuel F. B. Morse, the man who invented the Morse code, brought photography to America in the late 1830s. From his studio at the National Academy of Design in New York City, Morse taught the basics of photography. Many of his students documented the Civil War in photographs. Photography in the United States was in its infancy in 1861 when the Civil War began. By the time the war had ended four years later, photography had come of age.

The Civil War Is the First War to be Documented with Photos

Although a few photographs were taken during the Crimean War in the late 1850s, the American Civil War was the first in which photography played a major role. During the Civil War, photographers did not go into battle with the troops, as photo-journalists do today. They frequently rode out after a battle on the wagons that were going to collect the dead.

Cameras were bulky and very heavy. They used collodion-coated glass plates to record the images. Collodion is a thick substance made of plant fiber (cellulose) from cotton or wood that is treated with nitric acid and dissolved in alcohol or ether. The plates had to be sensitized in a chemical bath just before the picture was taken and developed immediately after exposure in a second chemical bath. It was awkward, painstaking work, but the resulting photos were remarkable.

Mathew Brady, the Most Famous Civil War Photographer

The best-known Civil War photographer was Mathew B. Brady. When he was eighteen years old, Brady was introduced to Samuel Morse and became one of his students. Brady was a quick learner who had a talent for photography. In 1844, he

Mathew Brady's wagon, which served as a roving photo studio during the Civil War, is pictured here outside Petersburg, Virginia, around 1864. Brady *(right)* won President Abraham Lincoln's approval to compile a photographic history of the war, but he did not secure any federal funds to finance the project.

opened a photography studio in New York City. He was soon recognized as one of America's greatest photographers. In 1856, he opened a second studio in Washington, D.C., in order to be closer to the people and events he wanted to photograph.

Although many Civil War photographs are attributed to Brady, most of them were taken by other people. Wishing to document the war in as much detail as possible, Brady hired photographers to do on-site photography. Brady spent most of his time supervising these photographers, preserving their negatives, and buying pictures taken by private photographers.

When printed, all of these photographs were attributed to Brady rather than to the people who took the pictures.

Brady's photographs were in great demand by newspapers and magazines during the war, but he was unable to sell them afterward. Most people did not want to be reminded of the horrors that had been endured by both sides. In 1875, a bankrupt Brady sold full title for his Civil War images to the United States

Some Civil War Statistics

It is estimated that 2,898,304 men and boys served in the Union army during the Civil War. The Confederate army was comprised of about 1,500,000 soldiers. In the Civil War, 360,000 Union and 260,000 Confederate soldiers died. These numbers are more than the combined total of deaths in all the other wars in which Americans have fought.

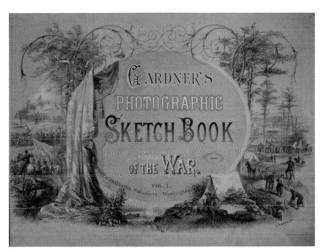

♦♦♦ **This is the title page of** *Gardner's Photographic Sketch Book of the Civil War.* **First published in 1866, the two-volume album includes 100 photographs.**

government for $25,000. At the time of his death, Brady was virtually unknown. Those who did remember him saw that he was buried at Arlington Cemetery, among the Civil War soldiers whom he had immortalized.

Timothy O'Sullivan and Alexander Gardner

Timothy O'Sullivan was one of the photographers who worked for Brady. He took his most famous photos in 1863 at the Battle of Gettysburg. Although the photographs were attributed to Brady, photos of that battle taken by O'Sullivan and later published in *Harper's Weekly* were thought to provide much of the inspiration for Abraham Lincoln's Gettysburg Address.

Alexander Gardner was another important Civil War photographer. When he immigrated to New York from Scotland in 1856, he found a job working in Brady's studio. He moved to

Washington, D.C., and managed Brady's Washington studio until 1862. He left that job to become the official photographer of the Army of the Potomac. He opened his own studio and gallery in Washington, D.C., where he photographed most of the officers of the Army of the Potomac. President Lincoln and many of his staff also sat for Gardner. Some of Gardner's most famous photos were taken at Lincoln's funeral in 1865. Gardner published a two-volume album of photographs in 1866 entitled *Photographic Sketch Book of the Civil War*.

Alfred Waud

Photos were not the only images documenting events of the war. Alfred Waud, a sketch artist, accompanied the troops to the front lines. At considerable risk to himself, he made detailed sketches as battles were occurring. These were published in many newspapers, as well as in *Harper's Weekly*. His sketches, unlike the photos of the time, captured the action of a battle rather than its aftermath.

Winslow Homer

Best known for his oil paintings of American life, Winslow Homer provided many images of the Civil War. He began his artistic training at nineteen as an apprentice to a lithographer in Boston. Homer moved to New York, where he studied at the National Academy of Design. While there, he supported himself by selling drawings to *Harper's Weekly*. Later, Homer was hired

Alfred Waud is captured sketching a scene on the battlefield in Gettysburg, Pennsylvania, in this photograph taken by Civil War photographer Timothy O'Sullivan in July 1863. Waud was born in London, England, in 1828. He immigrated to the United States in 1850.

by *Harper's* to provide sketches of the Civil War for publication in the magazine. Accompanying Union troops into battle, Homer made copious sketches, then returned to his New York studio to make his final drawings. Woodcuts made from his drawings were published in *Harper's* throughout the war. Unlike Waud's sketches, Homer's drawings dealt with camp life and other intimate views of the troops rather than scenes from battles. Using the sketches he made at the front, Homer also produced several important oil paintings depicting Civil War events. *Yankee Sharpshooter*, painted in 1862, and *Prisoners from the Front*, painted in 1865, are two of the most famous.

Stephen Crane undoubtedly had access to works by all of these artists. Newspapers and magazines published photos and sketches to illustrate their stories. As a journalist, Crane had easy access to them. By the time *The Red Badge of Courage* was published, Winslow Homer was quite famous. His paintings and the albums of photos produced by Gardner were available for Crane's study. The vivid pictures Crane produced with words undoubtedly originated, in part, from actual pictures of war produced by Brady, O'Sullivan, Gardner, Waud, Homer, and others. The images created by the photographers and artists who documented this war were so vivid that Crane could borrow and meld them into a powerful, believable story.

Chapter 4

Slavery and the Civil War

At the time of the American Revolution (1775–1782), which was fought to free the American colonies from the tyranny of British rule, slavery was legal in every colony. When the U.S. Constitution was written in 1787, slavery was not prohibited. Slavery was a fact of life not only in the original colonies but also in the states formed after the American Revolution.

As the population of the United States began to increase in the years following the American Revolution, many people moved to fertile farmland south of the Ohio River. Since there was a huge demand for cotton worldwide, it became the most important crop in the South. Large numbers of slaves were needed to work the cotton fields. Slavery was critical to the economic well-being of the South. The men who owned slaves were wealthy and politically powerful. Many of those elected to the federal House of Representatives and the Senate from Southern states were slave owners.

In contrast, the economy of the North was based on industry. Immigrants poured into the North from Europe and were hired,

◆◆◆ A group of slaves is shown preparing cotton for a cotton gin in 1862 on a plantation in Beaufort, South Carolina. Slavery was one of the main issues over which the Civil War was waged.

usually for little pay, to work in factories. With few exceptions, slaves held in Northern states were freed and incorporated into the Northern workforce.

The men of wealth and political power in the North were not slaveholders. Many of them believed that slavery was morally wrong and worked with other abolitionists to stop the spread of slavery in the United States. Most states north of the Ohio River were considered to be free states—ones in which slavery was not condoned.

The Fifth Amendment of the U.S. Constitution guarantees the protection of private property. Slaves were considered to be private property. In order to prohibit slavery in the United States, the Constitution would have to be altered to exclude slaves as property. Since the number of slave states in America was about equal to the number of free states, senators from slave states were successful in blocking amendments to the Constitution that would abolish slavery.

At the end of the Mexican-American War in 1847, vast areas in the West became available to be partitioned into states. The issue of whether slavery would be allowed in these territories led to political struggle between the North and the South. The struggle eventually led to war.

Strong Southern Presence in Federal Government

In "The War That Never Goes Away," an article published in *American Heritage* magazine in 1995, James McPherson wrote that from 1789 to 1861, two-thirds of the presidents of the United States were slaveholders from the South. Two-thirds of the speakers of the House and presidents pro tem of the Senate were also from the South. Twenty out of thirty-five Supreme Court justices were from the South. After the Civil War, a century passed before another Southerner was elected president.

To Dissolve or Preserve the Union

The Southern states believed so strongly about owning slaves and introducing slavery into Western territories that they were willing to cut their ties with Northern states. The moral issue perceived by the South was one of states' rights. Southerners felt they had the right to decide how to govern themselves and to decide what would be legal in their states. They felt that they had the right to withdraw from the Union.

The North was willing to go to war to stop the spread of slavery into the West. Northern states also had a vital interest in preserving the Union. They felt that if a state could secede whenever it chose to do so, the Union would soon fall apart, leaving,

♦♦♦ This South Carolina street banner from 1860 captures the defiance of the South in the face of federal pressure to end slavery.

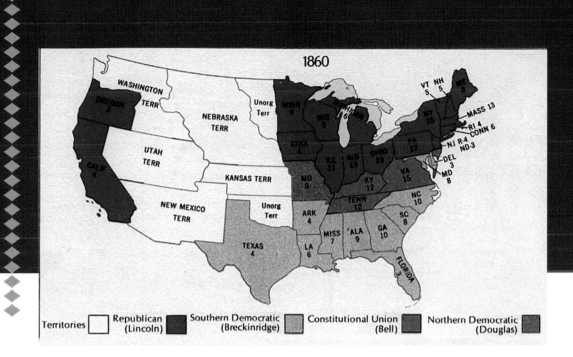

On this map showing the breakdown of electoral votes during the 1860 election, the rift between North and South can clearly be seen. The states won by Abraham Lincoln are indicated in red. Note that he didn't carry a single Southern state.

as Abraham Lincoln put it in a speech to Congress on July 4, 1861, "a multitude of petty, squabbling autocracies." To the North, preservation of the Union was worth any cost. The issue of actually freeing slaves did not arise until 1863, following Lincoln's Emancipation Proclamation.

War Follows Lincoln's Election to the Presidency

The presidential election of 1860 had a profound effect on the United States, which was already teetering on the brink of civil war. Abraham Lincoln had been selected as the presidential candidate of the newly formed Republican Party—a party comprised mainly of those who opposed the expansion of slavery. The Democratic Party was split between Northern Democrats, led by Senator Stephen Douglas of Illinois, and Southern Democrats, led by then Vice President John C. Breckenridge. At the Democratic National Convention, neither candidate could win the number of votes needed to be the party's candidate, so both ran for the presidency. A fourth candidate, Senator John

Soldiers of the Civil War

As many as 420,000 soldiers who fought in the Civil War were young boys. In *The Boys' War: Confederate and Union Soldiers Talk About the Civil War*, Jim Murphy writes that there was a large number of boys fighting who were sixteen years of age or younger. Since record-keeping was sloppy and enlistment procedures were poorly documented, no one knows the exact numbers. After the war, an army statistician estimated that between 10 and 20 percent of all soldiers were sixteen years old or younger. That would mean that between 250,000 and 420,000 boys fought in the war.

◆◆◆ This engraving, titled *Bombardment of Fort Sumter*, depicts the Confederate attack on the Union position that marked the start of the American Civil War. There were no casualties during the bombardment, but the Union forces were forced to surrender the fort within a day.

Bell of Tennessee, also ran, representing the Constitutional Union Party.

On Election Day, November 6, 1860, voter turnout was heavy. Eighty-one percent of eligible men voted. Neither women nor people of color were eligible to vote in that election.

Because of the split in the Democratic Party and the presence of a fourth-party candidate, Lincoln won the election. He got only 40 percent of the popular vote but carried 59 percent of the votes of the electoral college.

For the first time in the history of America, voters from defeated parties refused to accept the election results. Instead, they chose to secede, or withdraw, from the Union. South Carolina seceded on December 20, 1860, followed quickly by other Southern states. On February 9, 1861, the Confederate States of America was formed.

A month after Lincoln's inauguration, Confederate general Pierre Beauregard of South Carolina fired on Fort Sumter in Charleston, South Carolina. The war was on.

Chapter 5

Where It All Happened: The Battle of Chancellorsville

Stephen Crane did not identify the particular battle described in *The Red Badge of Courage*. His emphasis was on Henry's reaction to battle rather than the battle itself. There is no doubt, however, that Crane chose the Battle of Chancellorsville as the setting for *The Red Badge of Courage*. He says so in his short story, "The Veteran." In that story, an elderly Henry Fleming says,

> **Why in my first battle I thought the sky was falling down . . . The trouble was I thought they were all shooting at me . . . And it seemed so darn unreasonable, you know. I wanted to explain to 'em what an almighty good fellow I was, because I thought then they might quit all trying to hit me. But I couldn't explain, so they kept on being unreasonable—blim!—blam!—bang! So I run! . . . That was at Chancellorsville. Of course, afterwards, I got kind of used to it.**

A Stalemate

War had raged for two years before the Battle of Chancellorsville. In spite of forty-two major battles, a huge loss of life, and remarkable hardships, neither side was any closer to victory than it had been at the start of the war. In order for the North to win, it had to capture Richmond, Virginia, the capital of the Confederacy. The South, on the other hand, needed support from Great Britain and France to win. If it did not get that help, its only hope of winning was for the North to simply give up the fight—a very real possibility at that point in the conflict.

"Fighting Joe" Hooker Takes Over

In late 1862, the federal Army of the Potomac was soundly defeated at Fredericksburg, Virginia, by a much smaller Confederate force. President Lincoln, believing that the useless slaughter had been largely the fault of his generals, appointed Joseph "Fighting Joe" Hooker to command the Army of the Potomac. Over the next four months, General Hooker whipped the badly demoralized army into shape with hard work, repeated drilling, and attention to some of the complaints of the common soldiers—bad food and no furloughs or leaves of absence. By April 1863, the morale of the 134,000 men of the Army of the Potomac was much improved, as were their fighting skills.

◆◆◆ This portrait of General Joseph Hooker was taken sometime between 1860 and 1865, most likely during the Civil War. It is part of a collection of Mathew Brady's photographs of Civil War–era personalities at the National Archives.

After complicated journeyings with many pauses, there had come months of monotonous life in a camp. He [Henry] had had the belief that real war was a series of death struggles with small time in between for sleep and meals; but since his regiment had come to the field the army had done little but sit still and try to keep warm . . . Also he was drilled and drilled and reviewed and drilled and drilled and reviewed.

During this period, Hooker devised a plan by which he thought he could force General Robert E. Lee's Army of Northern Virginia away from its defensive sites around Fredericksburg. The plan included dividing the Army of the Potomac into three forces. The cavalry was to ride around Lee's forces and south toward Richmond to cut off communications and supplies passing between Richmond and Fredericksburg.

"The cavalry started this morning," he [the tall soldier] continued. "They say there ain't hardly any cavalry left in camp. They're going to Richmond, or some place, while we fight all the Johnnies [Confederate soldiers]."

A third of Hooker's infantry was to attack Fredericksburg directly and a third was to remain in reserve. Hooker himself was to lead the remaining men. They would cross the Rappahannock and Rapidan Rivers, skirt the left side of Lee's army, and attack the rear of Lee's defenses.

When another night came the columns, changed to purple streaks, filed across two pontoon bridges. A glaring fire wine-tinted the waters of the river. Its rays, shining upon the moving masses of troops, brought forth here and there sudden gleams of silver or gold. Upon the other shore a dark and mysterious range of hills was curved against the sky. The insect voices of the night sang solemnly.

Hooker's daring plan didn't work. His cavalry was slowed down by bad weather. The Confederate cavalry, which was

Sketched by Alfred Waud, this engraving depicts a division of the Army of the Potomac fighting in the woods in 1862. The Army of the Potomac was the part of the Union army that fought in the eastern United States during the Civil War. It was disbanded in 1865 at the end of the war.

patrolling the Rappahannock River, saw Hooker's troops crossing the river and immediately reported this to General Lee. In a bold move of his own, Lee left 9,000 men to keep an eye on the Union troops at Fredericksburg and took the rest of his men to stop General Hooker.

Chancellorsville Was Just a House

On the night of April 30, 1863, General Hooker's men camped at the edge of a dense woods known as the Wilderness of

Spotsylvania. Near their camp, standing at a road junction, was a large brick house owned by the Chancellor family. The house and a few outbuildings constituted Chancellorsville.

Absurd ideas took hold upon him [Henry]. He thought that he did not relish the landscape. It threatened him . . . A house standing placidly in distant fields had to him an ominous look. The shadows of the woods were formidable. He was certain that in this vista there lurked fierce-eyed hosts.

◆◆◆ This studio portrait of Confederate general Stonewall Jackson was taken in 1862, months before he was shot by friendly fire during the Civil War.

The next day, May 1, 1863, Hooker's men moved out of the woods into a clearing only to be met by General Lee's troops led by General Thomas "Stonewall" Jackson. Although General Hooker had many more men and more firepower than General Lee, he elected to pull back and to dig into a defensive position near Chancellorsville.

Later that day, Jeb Stuart, another well-known Confederate general, told General Lee and General Jackson that the right side of Hooker's army was unprotected.

The critical phase of the Battle of Chancellorsville occurred on May 2. General Jackson led 26,000 Confederates around the right side of Hooker's army. With only two hours of daylight remaining, Jackson attacked, sending soldiers of the Union's XI Corps retreating over 2 miles (3.2 kilometers) to the main body of Hooker's force at Chancellorsville.

Stonewall Falls

The aftermath of this daring raid, while leading to a victory for Lee at Chancellorsville, was a disaster for the Confederacy in the long run. While returning through unfamiliar territory in the dead of night, General Jackson and his staff were mistaken for Union soldiers by Confederate sentries and fired upon. General Jackson was hit in the right arm and later had the arm amputated. He died eight days later.

The Stalemate Continues

Had General Hooker launched a counterattack immediately, the outcome of the battle might have been different. The Confederate army was split in half with Hooker's army between the two halves. The Confederates were greatly out-numbered and without the leadership of Stonewall Jackson. But Hooker did not take advantage of the situation.

Assuming General Jackson's command, Jeb Stuart resumed the attack at daybreak, on May 3. He reunited the two parts of Lee's army and pushed the Army of the Potomac back toward the river. At the end of the day, Hooker's troops retreated across the river and the battle was over. The net result of the three days of fighting was 17,000 Union casualties, 13,000 Confederate casualties, and the loss of General Jackson. Neither side had gained an inch.

Chapter 6

Words of War

S ome authors are capable of creating the plot and characters of books set in an imaginary time or place. Stephen Crane could not do that. His book, set during the Battle of Chancellorsville in the Civil War, required that he use real people and real events to make his characters come to life. To craft *The Red Badge of Courage*, he appears to have drawn on stories heard in his youth, diaries and letters written by people who fought in the war, newspaper articles, books, and even the lessons taught by his teachers.

Students Research the 124th Regiment

The question of why Crane chose the Battle of Chancellorsville as the backdrop for his book is explained by Charles LaRocca in his 1991 article, "Stephen Crane's Inspiration," published in *American Heritage* magazine. LaRocca is a high school history teacher in Orange County, New York. He was sure that the 124th New York Volunteers, known as the Orange Blossoms, was the army unit on which Crane based his fictitious 304th New York Volunteers in

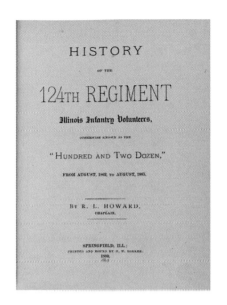

HISTORY
OF THE
124TH REGIMENT
Illinois Infantry Volunteers,
OTHERWISE KNOWN AS THE
"HUNDRED AND TWO DOZEN,"
FROM AUGUST, 1862, TO AUGUST, 1865.

BY R. L. HOWARD,
CHAPLAIN.

SPRINGFIELD, ILL.;
PRINTED AND BOUND BY H. W. ROKKER.
1880.

◆◆◆ **This is the title page of *History of the 124th Regiment N.Y.S.V.* (New York State Volunteers) by Colonel Charles Weygant. It was originally published in 1877.**

The Red Badge of Courage. To prove this, LaRocca directed a small group of students in a research project that spanned eight years. The students searched through regimental histories, Crane archives, and newspaper accounts, and they talked with historians and studied letters and diaries of Civil War soldiers. The results of the students' research constitute the information presented in LaRocca's article.

Crane Spent Boyhood Years in Orange County

One of the most significant findings of LaRocca's students was that Crane had spent several boyhood years in Port Jervis, New York, which is in Orange County. He was reported to have listened to the tales spun by veterans of the 124th New York Volunteers who lived in Port Jervis. Crane undoubtedly remembered many of those stories when he started his novel.

The 124th was made up of more than 1,000 boys and men. The first battle of the war in which they fought was the Battle

of Chancellorsville. In *The Red Badge of Courage*, Crane's 304th was made up almost exclusively of untried troops like the Orange Blossoms.

> "How do you think the reg'ment 'll do?" [Henry asked].
> "Oh, they'll fight all right, I guess after they once get into it," said the other [Jim] with cold judgment. "There's been heaps of fun poked at 'em because they're new, of course, and all that; but they'll fight all right, I guess."

♦♦♦ **Veterans of the 124th Regiment pose for a reunion photo at a monument erected in their honor in Gettysburg, Pennsylvania, in 1897. It is widely accepted that Stephen Crane used the stories of the New York State Volunteers who served in the 124th Regiment as the basis for *The Red Badge of Courage*.**

The students found another piece of documentation to support Crane's knowledge of the 124th. Colonel Charles Weygant wrote a history of the 124th New York Volunteers. When he died in 1909, his obituary was published in the *Newburgh* [New York] *News*. It said: "[I]t is . . . generally supposed that Col. Weygant's book suggested to Crane the writing of his most powerful story *The Red Badge of Courage*. Young Crane has a brother . . . in Port Jervis and the author spent much of his early manhood in that neighborhood. It is known that he was familiar with Col. Weygant's book."

The Red Badge

LaRocca says that the title of Crane's novel is another clue of the importance of the Orange Blossoms to the writing of *The Red Badge of Courage*. In the novel, the red badge is the wound that Henry Fleming receives when hit with a rifle swung by a fleeing Union soldier. The red badge was also the name given the Kearny patch, a red diamond worn by men of the First Division, III Corps, of the Army of the Potomac. General Philip Kearny had devised the badge so his men could be recognized in battle. The 124th was the only untried III Corps unit at Chancellorsville to wear the red badge. According to the students, there exist today two red patches worn by Private James Conklin at Chancellorsville. Although he survived the war, the students believe that James Conklin was the inspiration for the Jim Conklin character in the novel, Henry Fleming's fellow soldier who died.

Fleeing Soldier Delivers Red Badge

In an article entitled "That Was at Chancellorsville," Harold Hungerford wrote that the best-known event of the Battle of Chancellorsville was the rout of the Union XI Corps by Stonewall Jackson and his men. The attack occurred late in the day when the Union troops were starting to settle down for the night. Soldiers of the XI Corps were taken by surprise, panicked, and fled. It was after this attack that Stonewall Jackson was shot in the arm—the injury that subsequently led to his death.

LaRocca and his students think there is little doubt that the fleeing soldier who injures Henry Fleming represents one of the soldiers of the XI Corps who fled from Stonewall Jackson.

[Henry] saw dark waves of men come sweeping out of the woods and down through the fields. He knew at once that the steel fibers had been washed from their hearts . . . they charged down on him like terrified buffaloes . . . soon he was in the midst of them. They were leaping and scampering all about him. Their blanched faces shone in the dusk . . . the youth finally clutched a man by the arm . . . he [the man] adroitly and fiercely swung his rifle. It crushed upon the youth's head. The man ran on.

The actual event was described by John W. Pitts in a letter to his brother dated September 8, 1863.

The 28th of April we marched about 8 miles down the river; the army was crossing in two places, below and above Fredericksburgh . . . On the 30th we were ordered to the right. We started about 2 PM, taking a roundabout way, so that the rebs would not see us, and marched till 2 o'clock that night when we halted. Early next morning found us again on the march. We crossed the river and

marched out to the front . . . the afternoon of May 2nd, General Hooker was shoving forward our lines when Stonewall Jackson threw his massed troops against the 11th Corps and they broke and got in our rear.

Other Sources of Information and Inspiration

In addition to accounts of the exploits of the 124th New York Volunteers garnered from veterans' tales, Colonel Weygant's book, and letters from veterans, Crane also consulted other Civil War histories. Thomas Beers, in an early biography of Crane, said that he used *Battles and Leaders of the Civil War* written in 1884 in preparation for writing *The Red Badge of Courage*. This book is a collection of memories by Union and Confederate officers. The accounts of battle strategies and the technical aspects of battle highlighted in this book would have been helpful background material for a person who had never seen war.

Stanley Wertheim, in a report to the Crane Society, wrote the following:

In his background reading for *The Red Badge of Courage*, Crane undoubtedly encountered some published personal narratives by Union veterans who had seen action in the ranks such as Wilber F. Hinman's *Corporal Si Klegg and His Pard* or Warren Lee Goss's

◆◆◆ In this letter Joseph Hoag Johnston, a 124th New York Volunteer, tells his mother about some of the activities that take place in the camps. Some of the passages in *The Red Badge of Courage* resemble the type of discussions that took place in letters between Civil War soldiers in the field and their families at home.

popular *Recollections of a Private/A Story of the Army of the Potomac* (1890). These memoirs traced the development of a recruit into a veteran. Crane most likely set out to write such a narrative.

Authenticity of Henry Fleming's Experiences

Thoughts and words of the boys who went to war reinforce the authenticity of Henry Fleming's behavior. In *The Boys' War: Confederate and Union Soldiers Talk About the Civil War*, Jim Murphy recorded these words of Elisha Stockwell, a fifteen-year-old Union soldier from Wisconsin.

I want to say, as we lay there and the shells were flying over us, my thoughts went back to my home, and I

thought what a foolish boy I was to run away and get into such a mess as I am in. I would have been glad to have seen my father coming after me.

In the first chapter of *The Red Badge of Courage*, Crane records Henry Fleming's thoughts.

He wished, without reserve, that he was at home again making the endless rounds from the house to the barn, from the barn to the house . . . He told himself that he was not formed for a soldier.

Elisha Stockwell's first battle could have described Henry Fleming's experience. Stockwell wrote the following in his diary:

The road was full for several rods and I shot for the middle of the [charging] crowd and began reloading. But as they were getting so close, I looked behind me to see what the rest [of my friends] were doing. I saw the Colors going out of sight over the hill, and only two or three men in sight. As I started to run, I heard several shouts, "halt!" . . . but I hadn't any thought of obeying them.

This is how Henry Fleming's first battle went.

A man near him who up to this time had been working feverishly at his rifle suddenly stopped and ran with howls . . . Others began to scamper away through the smoke. The youth turned his head . . . He saw the few fleeting forms. He yelled then with fright and swung about . . . Directly he began to speed toward the rear in great leaps . . . He ran like a blind man.

Classic Horrors of War

The Red Badge of Courage has remained in print since 1895. With its gritty pictures of war, it can be read in many ways. Many people believe that Henry is unchanged by his war experience. While he fights bravely in later skirmishes, he is motivated to do so because he wants others to think well of him. He is deluded into thinking that these actions "make him a man." Other readers choose to accept the story at face value—to enjoy it for its vivid descriptions. Some readers dig for meaning.

It is a classic work of American literature because Stephen Crane portrayed a terrible time in American history in a way that remains vivid, moving, and thought provoking. The smell, the noise, the dirt, and the blood that confronted Henry are still fresh, waiting to carry the reader back in time. The horrors of the American Civil War are the horrors of all wars.

Glossary

abolitionist   A person who favors doing away with slavery.

bohemian   One who is unconventional in life and habits, especially an artist, a writer, or a musician.

colors   An identifying badge, pennant, or flag.

demoralize   To weaken the spirit, courage, or discipline of someone.

electoral college   A group of people elected by voters to do the formal duty of electing the president and vice president of the United States.

freelance   Someone who works independent of any one company; also can describe the work done by someone who works by contract.

lithographer   An artist who uses a flat stone or plate, grease, water, and ink to make a print or picture.

president pro tem   A temporary president; the person who presides over the Senate in the vice president's absence.

proclamation   An official announcement.

rout   An overwhelming defeat.

skirmish   A brief fight between small groups, usually part of a larger battle or war.

tuberculosis   An infectious disease involving the lungs and other organs of the body.

tyranny   Very cruel and unjust use of power; oppressive or unjust government.

unabridged   A complete book or article; not shortened or condensed.

For More Information

Albert and Shirley Small Special Collection Library
University of Virginia
P.O. Box 400498
Charlottesville, VA 22903-2498
(434) 924-3025

The Civil War Preservation Trust
1331 H Street NW, Suite 1001
Washington, DC 20005
(202) 367-1861
e-mail: info@civilwar.org
Web site: http://www.civilwar.org

Fredericksburg and Spotsylvania National Military Park
120 Chatham Lane
Fredericksburg, VA 22405
(540) 786-2880 (Chancellorsville Visitors Center)
Web site: http://www.nps.gov/frsp

Web Sites

Due to the changing nature of Internet links, the Rosen
Publishing Group, Inc., has developed an online list of Web
sites related to the subject of this book. This site is updated
regularly. Please use this link to access the list:

http://www.rosenlinks.com/lal/rebc

For Further Reading

Asimov, Isaac. *Our Federal Union: The United States from 1816–1865.* Boston: Houghton Mifflin Co., 1975.

Catton, Bruce. *A Stillness at Appomattox.* Garden City, NY: Doubleday and Co., 1955.

Crane, Stephen. *Prose and Poetry.* New York: Literary Classics of the U.S., 1984.

Foote, Shelby. *The Civil War: A Narrative—Fredericksburg to Meridian.* New York: Vintage Books, 1986.

McPherson, James. *The Negro's Civil War: How American Blacks Felt and Acted During the War for the Union.* New York: Ballantine Books, 1991.

Meredith, Roy. *Mr. Lincoln's Camera Man, Mathew B. Brady.* New York: Charles Scribner's Sons, 1946.

Wertz, Jay, and Edwin Bearss. *Smithsonian's Great Battles and Battlefields of the Civil War.* New York: William Morrow and Co., 1997.

Bibliography

Crane, Stephen. *The Red Badge of Courage.* Cambridge, MA: Riverside Press, 1960.

Gibson, Donald B. *The Red Badge of Courage: Redefining the Hero* (Twayne's Masterwork Studies No. 15). Boston: Twayne Publishers, 1988.

Hayes, K. "How Stephen Crane Shapes Henry Fleming." *Studies of the Novel*, Fall 1990, pp. 296–308.

Hungerford, Harold. "'That Was at Chancellorsville': The Factual Framework of *The Red Badge of Courage*," *American Literature*, January 1963, Volume 34, Issue 4.

Kincheloe, H. "The Red Badge of Courage." *2,010 Plot Stories and Essay Reviews from the World's Fine Literature.* Frank McGill and Dayton Kohler, eds. Englewood Cliffs, NJ: Salem Press, 1976, pp. 5468–5472.

Mitchell, Lt. Col. Joseph B. *Decisive Battles of the Civil War.* New York: G. P. Putnam's Sons, 1955.

Murphy, Jim. *The Boys' War: Confederate and Union Soldiers Talk About the Civil War.* New York: Clarion Books, 1990.

Wertheim, Stanley, ed. *The Correspondence of Stephen Crane.* New York: Columbia University Press, 1999.

Primary Source Image List

Page 5: *Incidence of War—A Harvest of Death,* photograph of Civil War casualties by Mathew Brady. Housed at the Library of Congress Prints and Photographs Division in Washington, D.C.

Page 7 (left): Photograph of Jonathan Townley Crane, taken in the 1870s. Housed at Syracuse University.

Page 7 (right): Photograph of Mary Peck Crane, 1889. Housed at Syracuse University.

Page 8: Stephen Crane's grade records at Lafayette College from September 1890 to June 1892. Housed at the David Bishop Skillman Library at Lafayette College in Easton, Pennsylvania.

Page 8 (inset): Photograph of a cadet group (including Stephen Crane) taken around 1889 at Claverack College and Hudson River Institute in Columbia County, New York. Housed at the Newark Museum.

Page 9: Cover of Stephen Crane's first novel, *Maggie: A Girl of the Streets*, published in 1892. Housed at the David Bishop Skillman Library at Lafayette College in Easton, Pennsylvania.

Page 12: Undated photograph of Stephen Crane.

Page 15: Illustrated page from Warren Lee Goss's *Recollections of a Private.* Housed at the New York Public Library.

Page 17: *Attack on the Union Position at the Chancellorsville House, 1863,* drawing by Edwin Forbes. Housed at the Library of Congress Prints and Photographs Division in Washington, D.C.

Page 19: Photograph of wounded soldiers, taken on May 2, 1863, after the Battle of Chancellorsville. Part of a collection of Civil War photos at the National Archives in College Park, Maryland.

Page 27: Photograph of Mathew Brady's photography studio at Petersburg, Virginia, during the Civil War, circa 1864. Housed at the Library of Congress Prints and Photographs Division in Washington, D.C.

Page 27 (inset): Photograph of Civil War photographer Mathew Brady in 1861. Housed at the Library of Congress Prints and Photographs Division in Washington, D.C.

Page 31: Photograph of Alfred R. Waud sketching in the battlefield in Gettysburg, Pennsylvania, in July 1863. Taken by Timothy H. O'Sullivan. Housed at the Library of Congress Prints and Photographs Division in Washington, D.C.

Page 34: Photograph, taken by Timothy H. O'Sullivan, of slaves preparing cotton for the gin on a plantation in Beaufort, South Carolina, in 1862.

Page 42: Photograph of General Joseph Hooker, taken by Mathew Brady between 1860 and 1865. Housed at the National Archives in College Park, Maryland.

Page 44: *The Army of the Potomac—Kearney's Division Fighting in the Woods, Monday, June 30,* wood engraving after an original sketch by Alfred R. Waud. Published in *Harper's Weekly* on August 9, 1862. Housed at the Library of Congress in Washington, D.C.

Page 45: Portrait of General Thomas "Stonewall" Jackson, photographed around 1862.

Page 49: Title page of *History of the 124th Regiment N.Y.S.V.*, published in 1877.

Pages 50–51: Photograph of Civil War veterans at the 124th Monument in Gettysburg, Pennsylvania, in 1897. Housed at the New York State Military Museum and Veterans Research Center.

Page 55: Letter, dated September 18, 1862, from Joseph Johnston to his mother. Housed at the Huguenot Historical Society in New Paltz, New York.

Index

About the Author

Linda Bickerstaff, Ph.D., a retired surgeon, writes from her home in Ponca City, Oklahoma.

Photo Credits

Cover (top), p. 12 © Bettmann/Corbis; cover (bottom left), pp. 5, 17, 27, 29, 31, 44, 45 Library of Congress Prints and Photographs Division; cover (bottom right) courtesy of the Rare Books and Manuscripts Collection, New York Public Library, Astor, Lenox, and Tilden Foundations; p. 7 Stephen Crane Papers, Syracuse University Library, Special Collections Research Center; pp. 8 (inset), 9 Lafayette College Special Collections and Archives; p. 8 (back) Collection of the Newark Museum, Gift of Mr. G. Archer Crane; p. 15 General Research Division, New York Public Library, Astor, Lenox, and Tilden Foundations; pp. 19, 42 Record Group 111: Records of the Office of the Chief Signal Officer Still Picture Branch, National Archives and Records Administration; p. 34 © Corbis; pp. 36, 39 © North Wind Picture Archives; p. 37 http://teachpol.tcnj.edu; p. 49 General Research Division, New York Public Library, Astor, Lenox, and Tilden Foundations; pp. 50–51 New York State Military Museum p. 55 letter (detail), Joseph Hoag Johnston to Lettita Clark Johnston, September 18, 1862, The Joseph Hoag Johnston Civil War Papers (1855–1936), Huguenot Historical Society Library and Archives, New Paltz, New York, Mss Collections.

Design: Les Kanturek; Editor: Jill Jarnow; Photo Researcher: Rebecca Anguin-Cohen